music medals
Singing 20 two-part songs

Contents

Level	Title	Composer	Page
Copper	Little Waves	Lin Marsh	2
	Boots 'n' Cats	Francis Winston	3
	Beach Barbecue	Joseph Atkins	4
	Wiggle Your Toes	Niki Davies	6
	Travelling	Lin Marsh	8
	Let's Recycle!	Joseph Atkins	10
	Ready to Strike	Emily Barden	11
	Clouds	Lin Marsh	14
	Dancing Day!	Emily Barden	17
Bronze	The wind blows the seed	Lin Marsh	20
	Big, Silver Moon	Niki Davies	21
	Cheeky Monkey	Francis Winston	24
	Fire	Lin Marsh	25
	Brand New Day	Niki Davies	28
	Arirang	Trad. Korean	32
	What would it be like?	Emily Barden	33
	Lullaby	Niki Davies	36
	Perica	Trad. Chilean	38
	I Love Football	Francis Winston	39
	Igama la Bantwana	Trad. South African (Zulu)	40

Little Waves

Words and Music by
Lin Marsh

* Sing this song as a round, with Copper 2 starting when Copper 1 reaches '2' at bar 5. Two further singers can be added at intervals of two bars (these singers will not be assessed).

© 2025 by The Associated Board of the Royal Schools of Music

Boots 'n' Cats

Words and Music by
Francis Winston

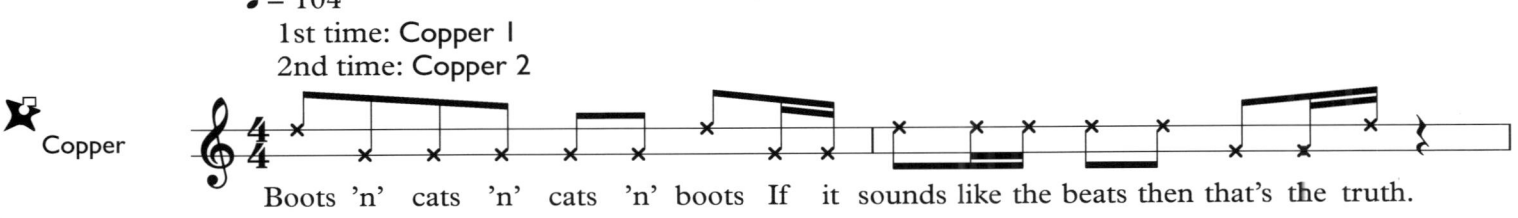
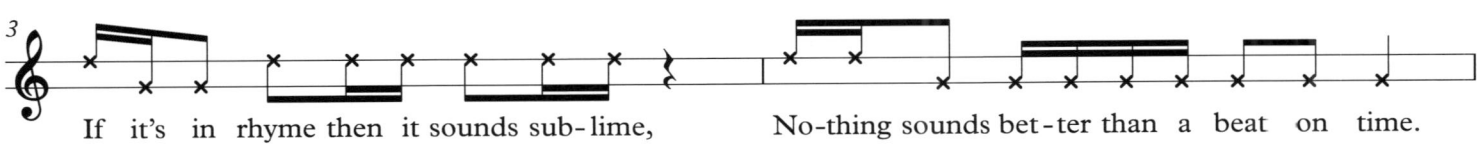
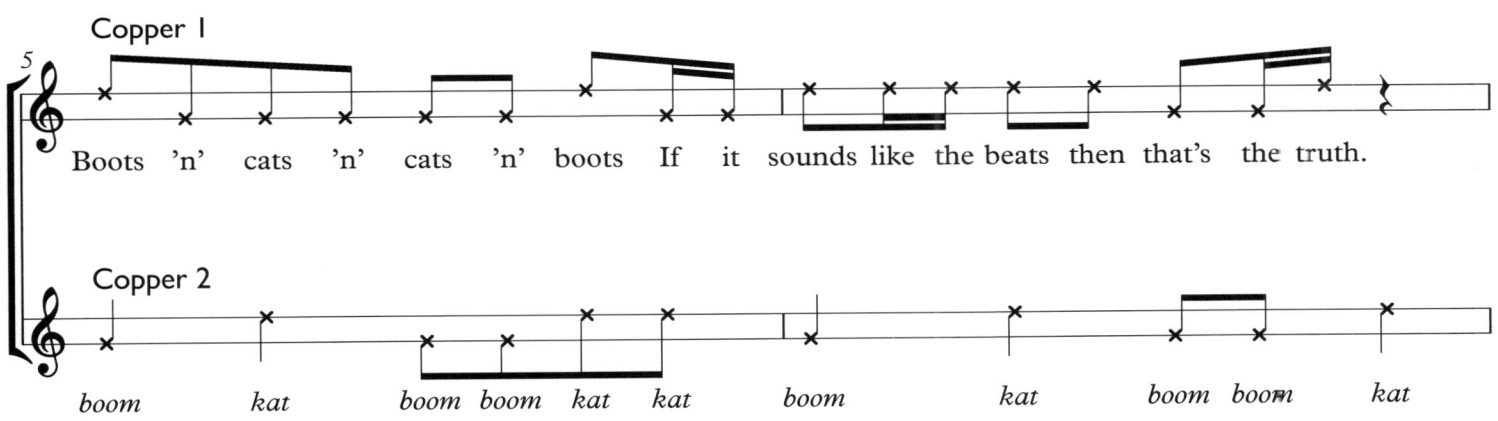
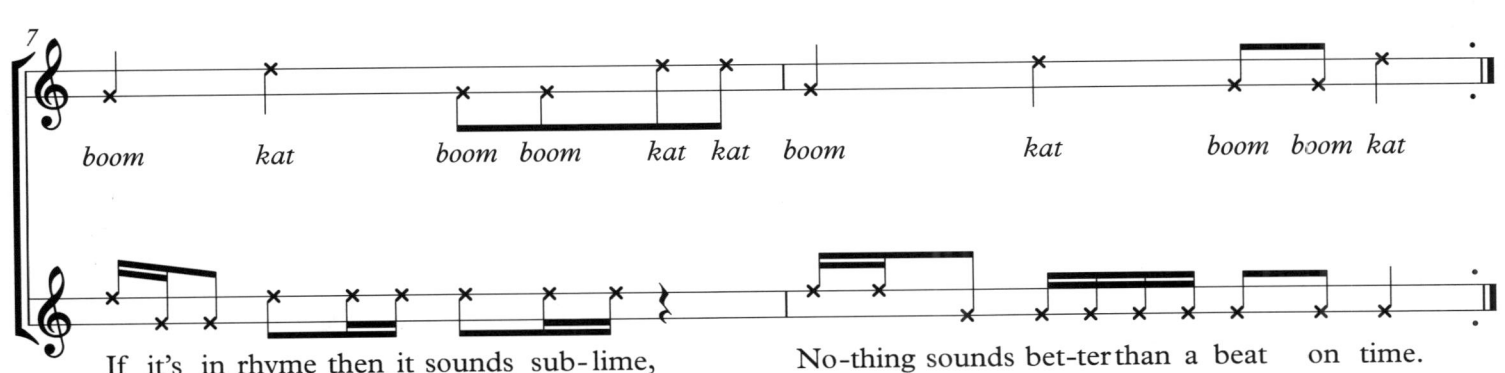

This rap has been notated on a two-line stave to give a sense of how the voice should be inflected for a stylistic performance. To listen to an audio demo, scan the QR code at the front of the book.

© 2025 by The Associated Board of the Royal Schools of Music

Beach Barbecue

Words and Music by
Joseph Atkins

Calypso groove ♩ = c.130

Copper 1: Join in our par-ty on the sand, Dance to the rhy-thm of the band.

Copper 2: Join in our par-ty on the sand, Dance to the rhy-thm of the band.

Sun-shine is out and the sky is blue; Some-thing smells good on the bar-be-cue!

Sun-shine is out and the sky is blue; Some-thing smells good on the bar-be-cue!

Chick-en is siz-zl-ing, Ea-sy on the spice!

Hot sauce is driz-zl-ing, Ea-sy on the spice!

© 2025 by The Associated Board of the Royal Schools of Music

Wiggle Your Toes

Words and Music by
Niki Davies

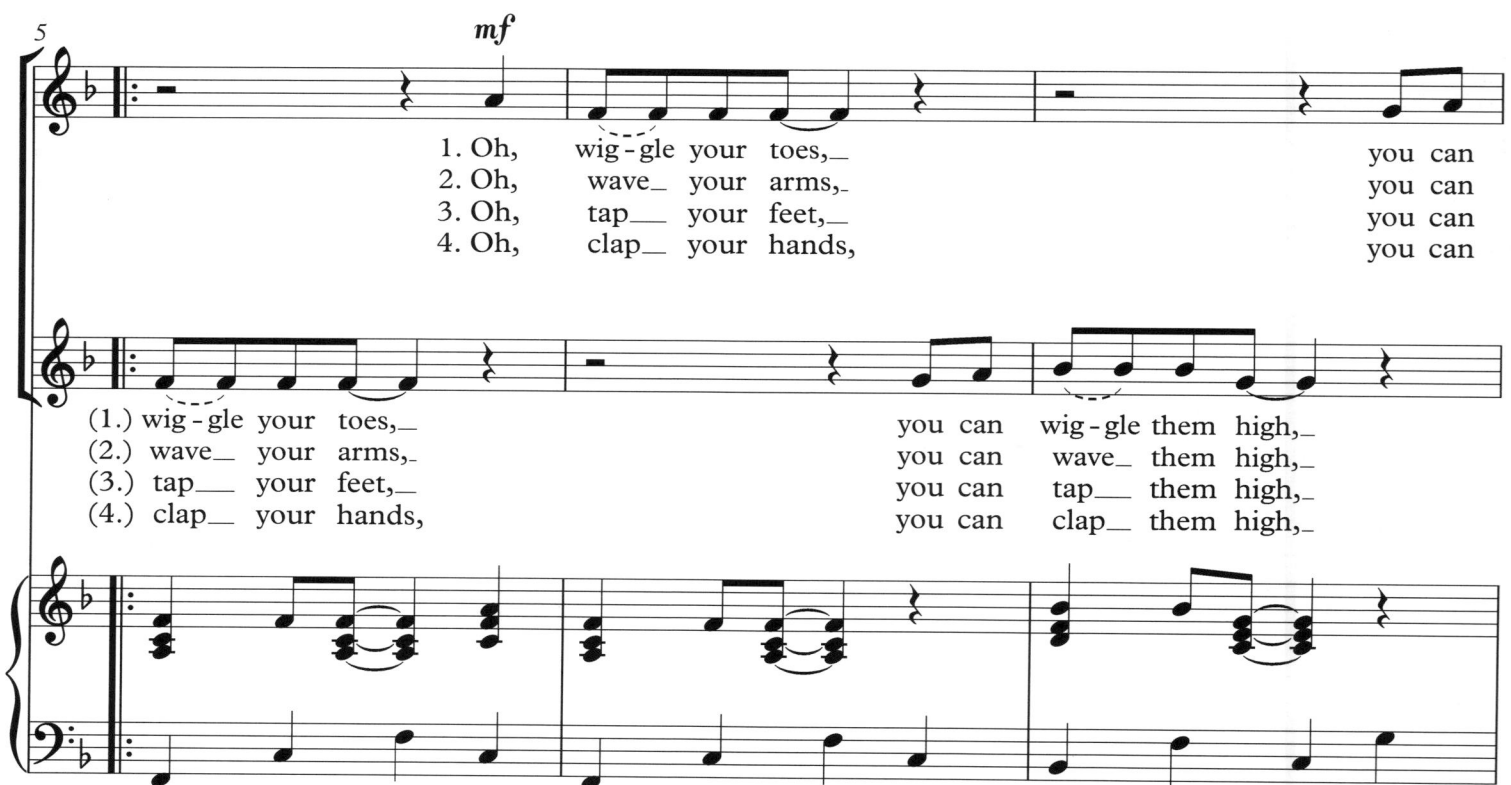

1. Oh, wig-gle your toes, you can wig-gle them high,
2. Oh, wave your arms, you can wave them high,
3. Oh, tap your feet, you can tap them high,
4. Oh, clap your hands, you can clap them high,

Copyright © 2025 The School Musicals Company Ltd

Travelling

Words and Music by
Lin Marsh

With movement ♩ = 100

1. Let's tra-vel by car, Let's tra-vel by train,
(2.) boat, Let's take a can - oe,
(3.) bus, Let's tra-vel by bike,

1. Let's tra-vel by car, Let's tra-vel by
2. Let's tra-vel by boat, Let's take a can -
3. Let's tra-vel by bus, Let's tra-vel by

Or we could fly In a rock-et or
Or we could cruise Just en-joy-ing the
Or find a friend And set off on a

train, Or we could fly
-oe, Or we could cruise
bike, Or find a friend

© 2025 by The Associated Board of the Royal Schools of Music

Let's Recycle!

Words and Music by Joseph Atkins

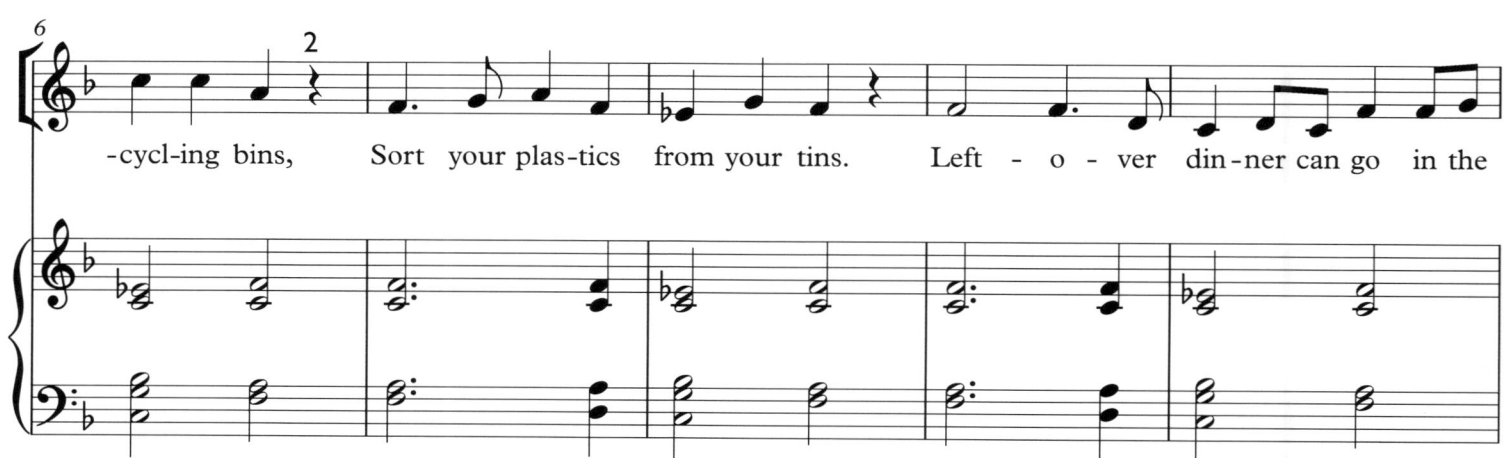
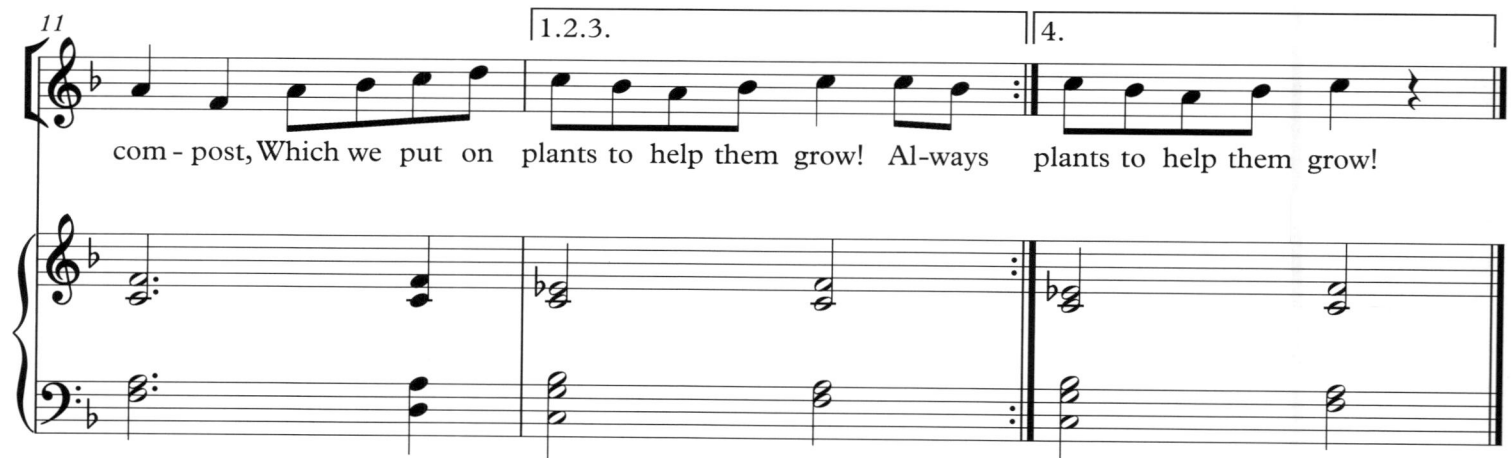

* Sing this song as a round, with Copper 2 starting when Copper 1 reaches '2'.

© 2025 by The Associated Board of the Royal Schools of Music

Ready to Strike

Words and Music by
Emily Barden

© 2025 by The Associated Board of the Royal Schools of Music

Clouds

Words and Music by
Lin Marsh

With movement ♩ = 104

Copper 1, Copper 2, Piano

Lyrics:
Cu-mu-lus and nim-bus, cir-rus and stra-tus,
Blown by the breeze, how you dance and you fly.
Blown by the breeze, how you dance and you fly.

© 2025 by The Associated Board of the Royal Schools of Music

Dancing Day!

Words and Music by
Emily Barden

© 2025 by The Associated Board of the Royal Schools of Music

The wind blows the seed

Words and Music by
Lin Marsh

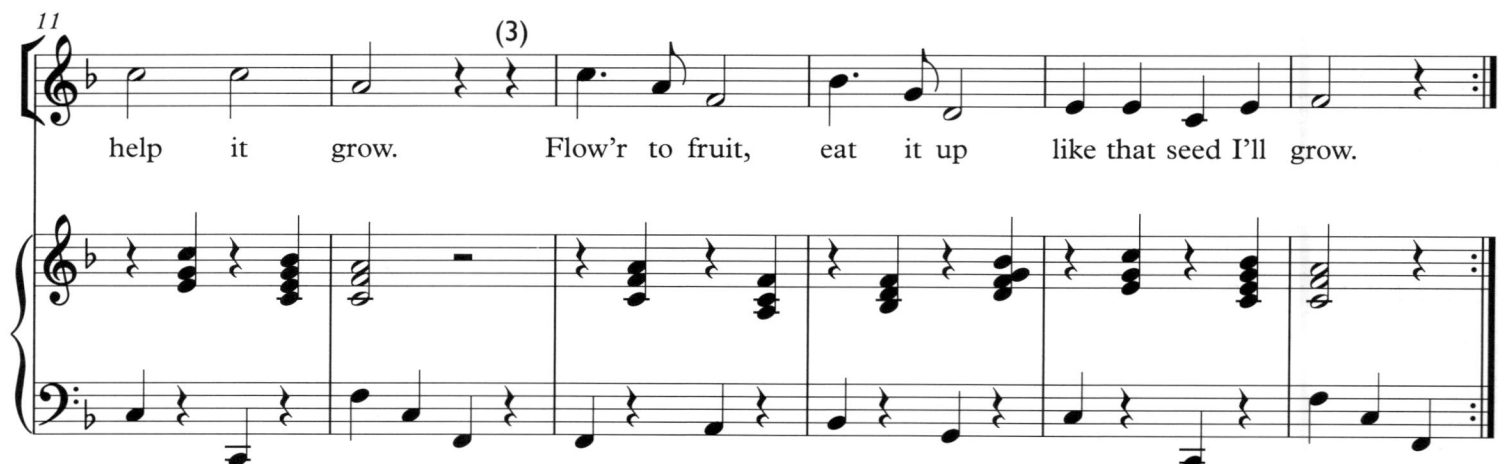

* Sing this song as a round, with Copper 2 starting when Copper 1 reaches '2' in bar 8. An optional 3rd singer may begin when Copper 1 reaches '3' in bar 12 (3rd singer will not be assessed).

© 2025 by The Associated Board of the Royal Schools of Music

Big, Silver Moon

Words and Music by
Niki Davies

Copyright © 2025 The School Musicals Company Ltd

Cheeky Monkey

Words and Music by
Francis Winston

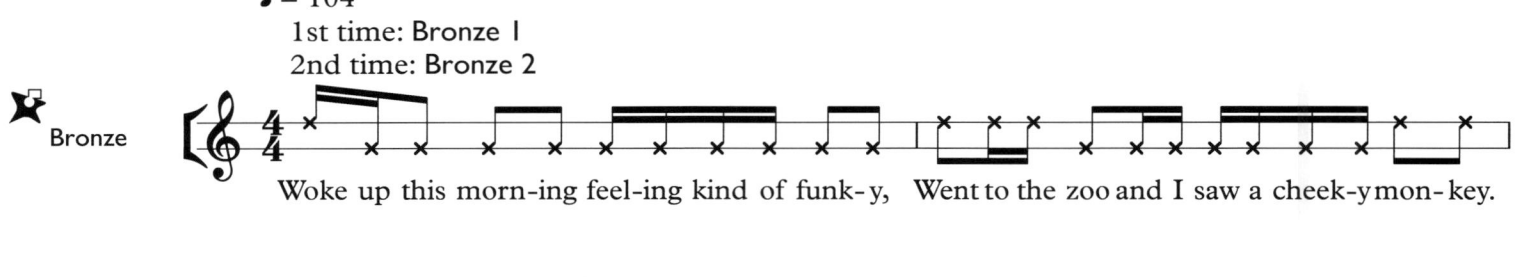

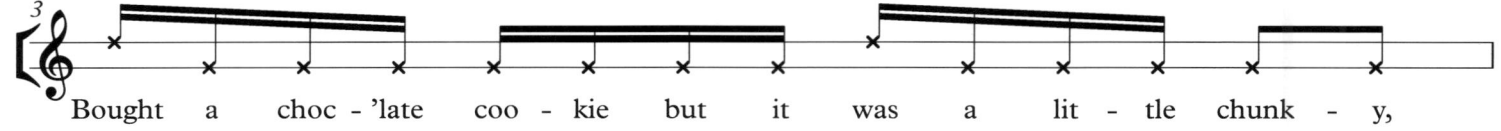

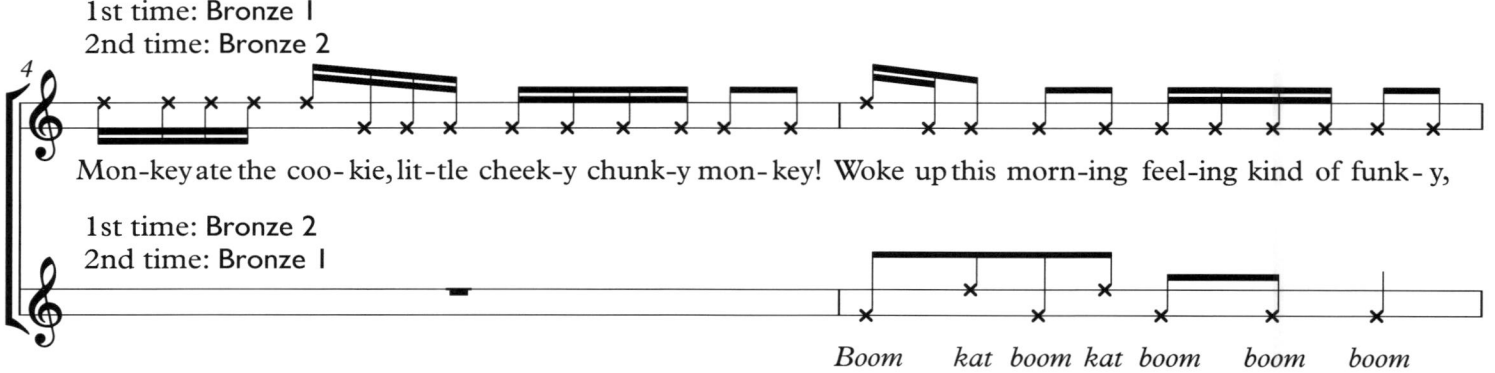

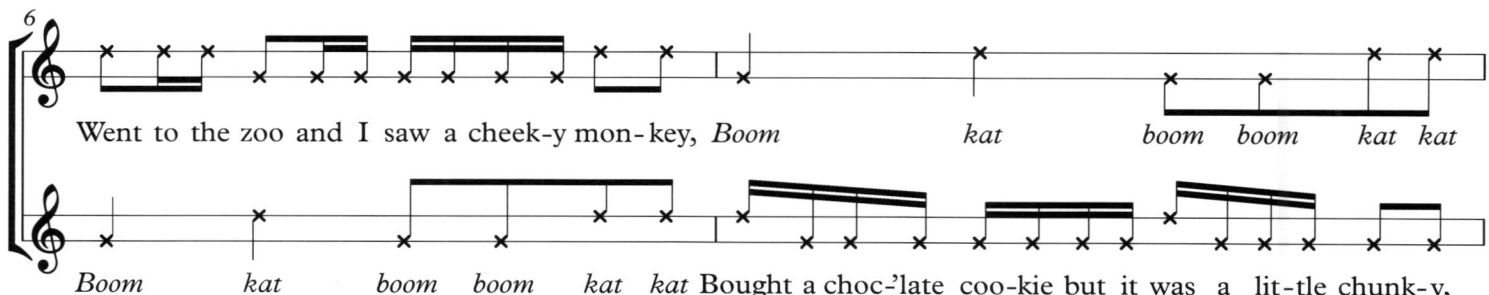

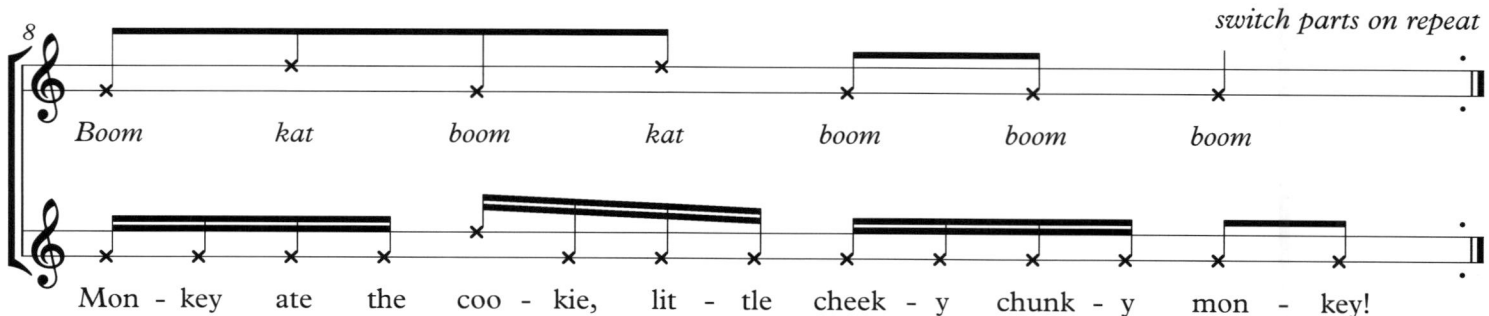

This rap has been notated on a two-line stave to give a sense of how the voice should be inflected for a stylistic performance. To listen to an audio demo, scan the QR code at the front of this book.

© 2025 by The Associated Board of the Royal Schools of Music

Timeline

America		Europe
	1517	Luther's Reformation begins
	1534	Henry VIII separates the Church of England from Rome
	1540	Jesuit Order established
	1545	Council of Trent convened to reform the Catholic Church
	1547	Edward VI to English throne Protestantization of Church of England
	1553	Mary Tudor attempts to restore Roman Catholicism in England "Marianist Priests"
	1558	Elizabeth I demands church uniformity: "Recusants" and "Church Papists" resist; English Roman Catholic colleges and convents established in Europe: "seminary priests" return to England; RC underground
	1581	Edmund Campion executed
1584 Ill-fated Roanoke Island settlement in Virginia Colony		
	1603	James I (Stuart), King of England; Protestantization
	1605	Gunpowder Plot; Anti-Catholic reaction
1607 Jamestown established in Virginia Colony		
	1611	Ulster (Protestant) Plantation in nine northern Irish counties
1619 Virginian House of Burgesses convened		
1620 *Mayflower* settlement in Massachusetts		
	1624	Lord Baltimore converts to Catholicism

Fire

Words and Music by
Lin Marsh

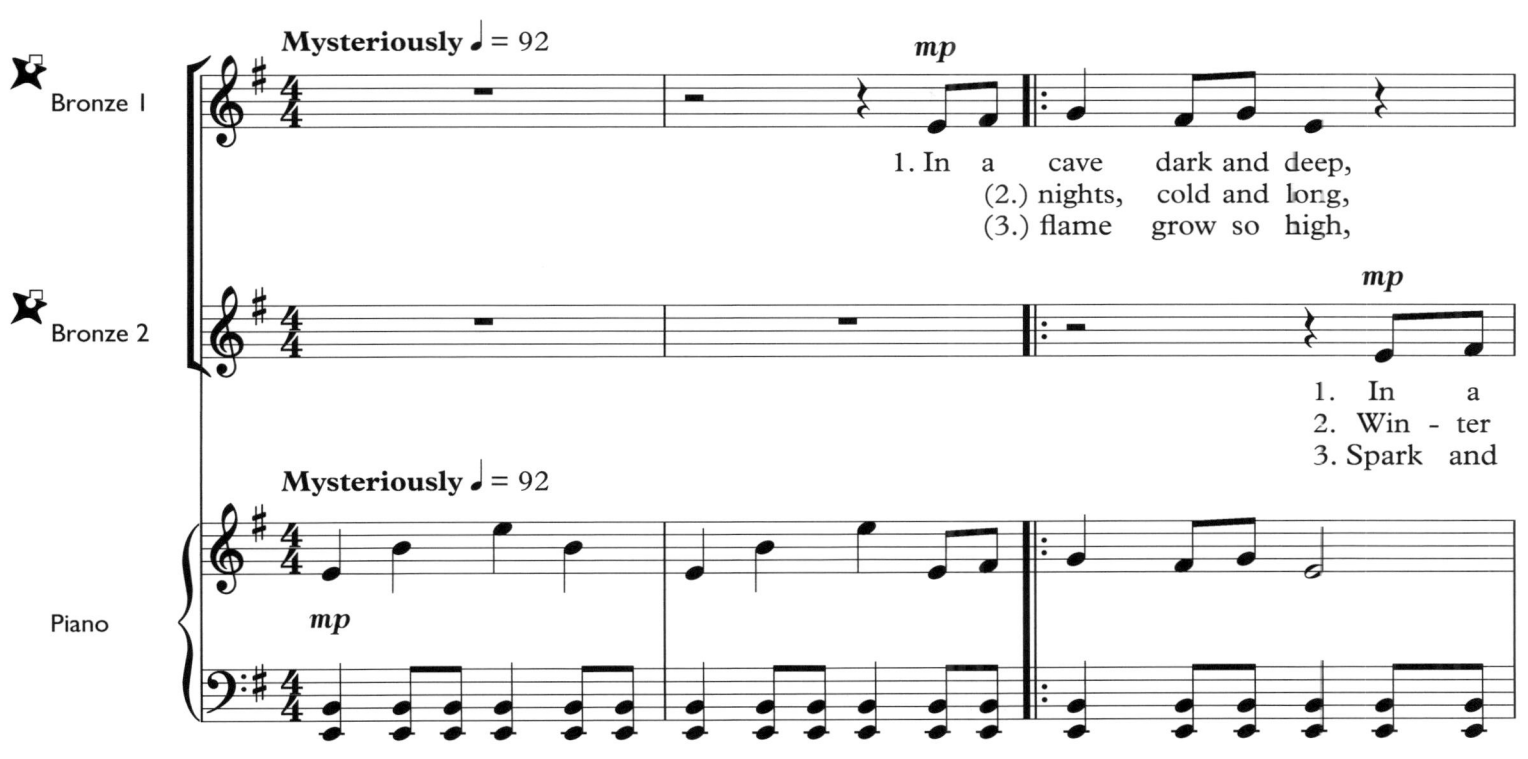
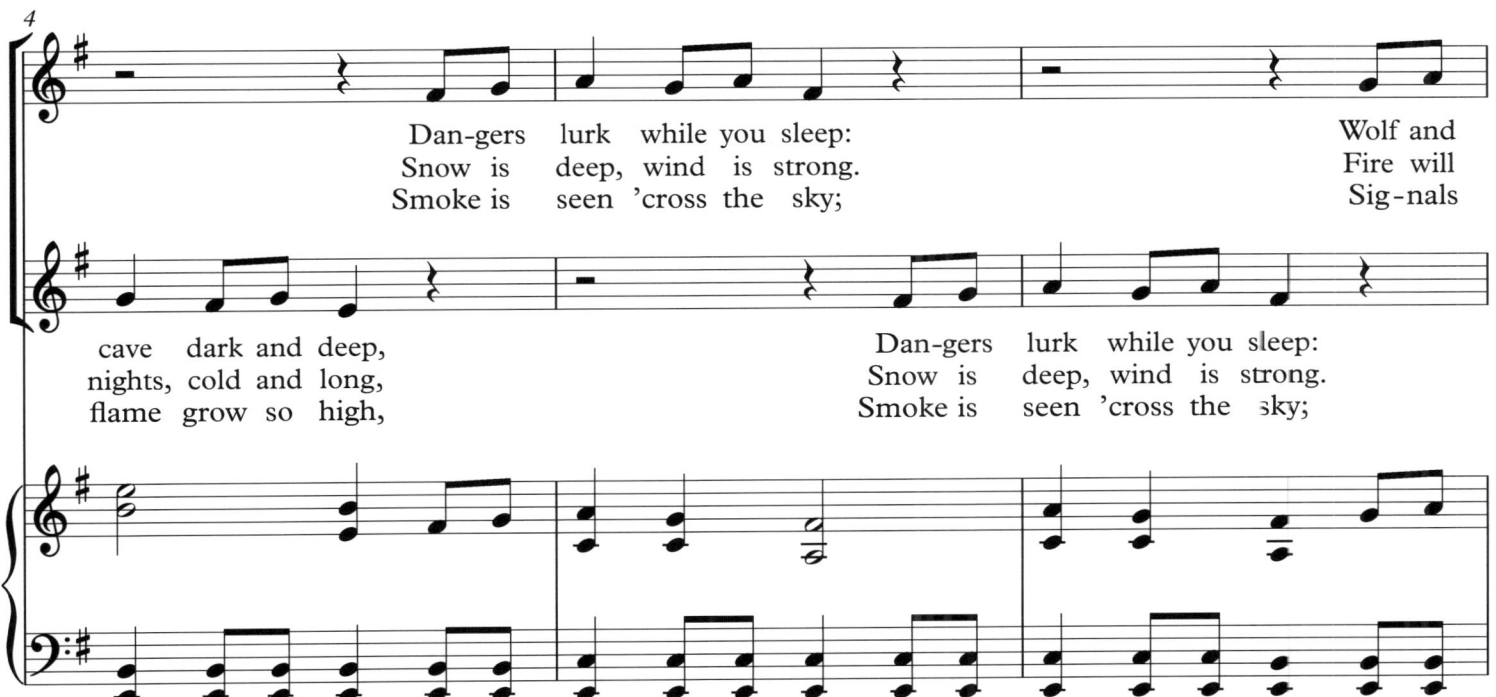

© 2025 by The Associated Board of the Royal Schools of Music

Brand New Day

Words and Music by
Niki Davies

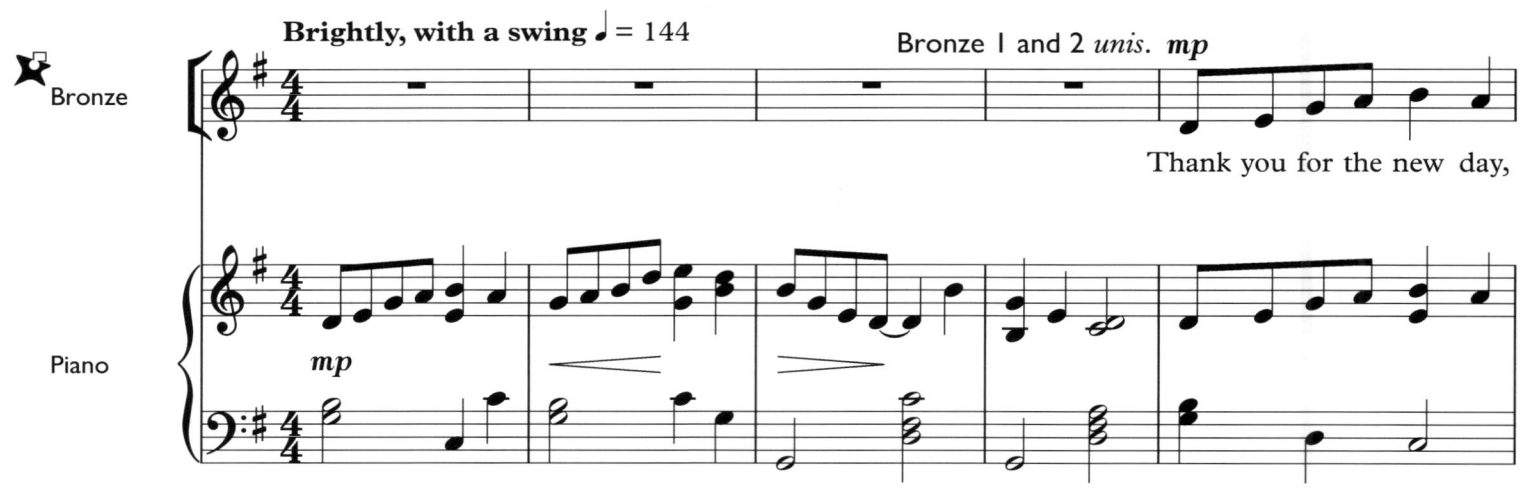

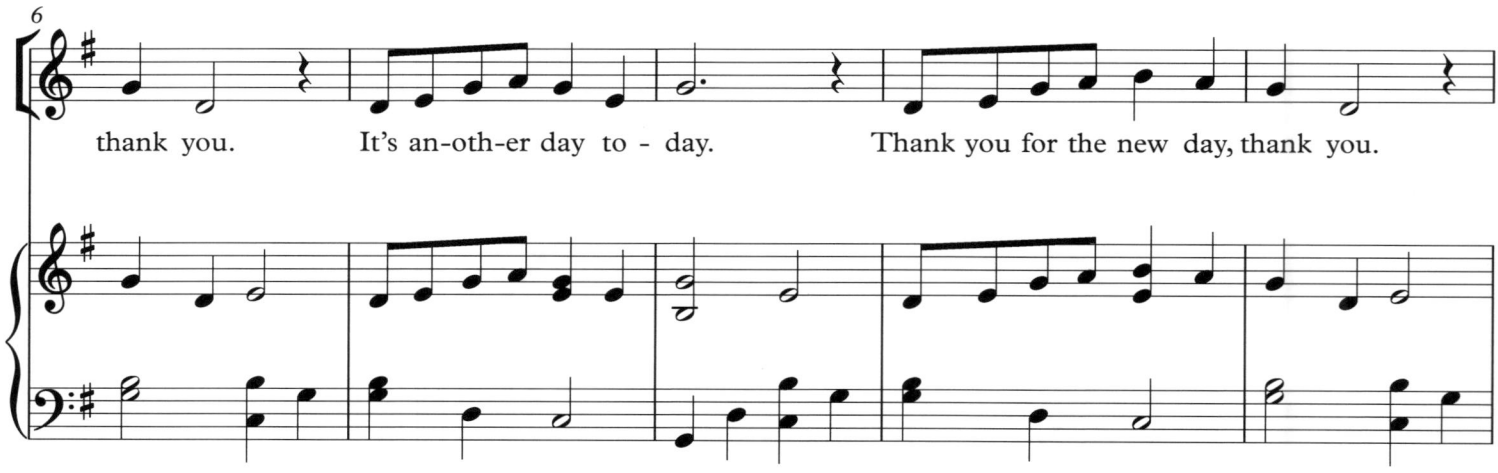

Copyright © 2025 The School Musicals Company Ltd

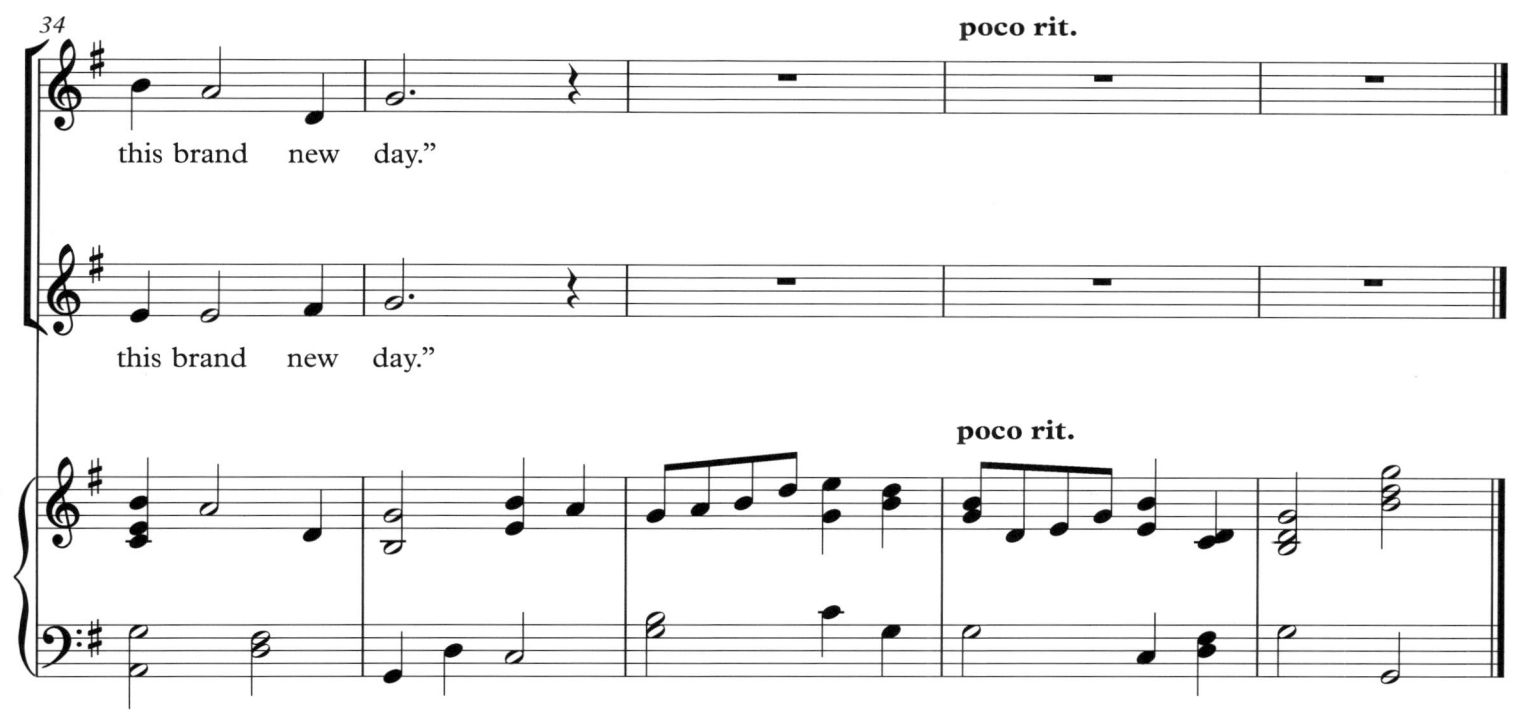

Arirang

Trad. Korean

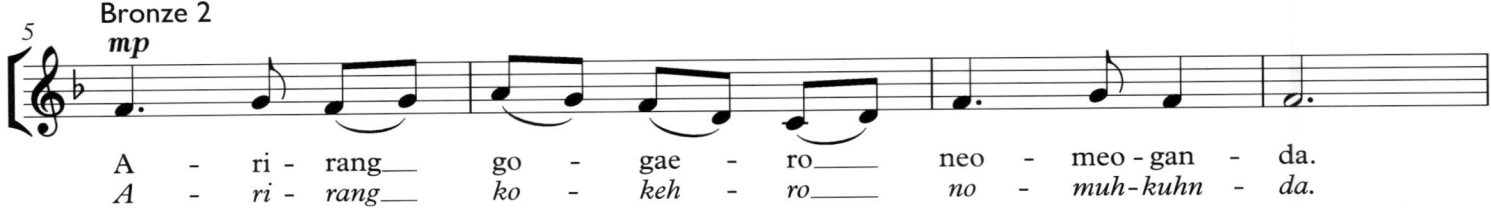

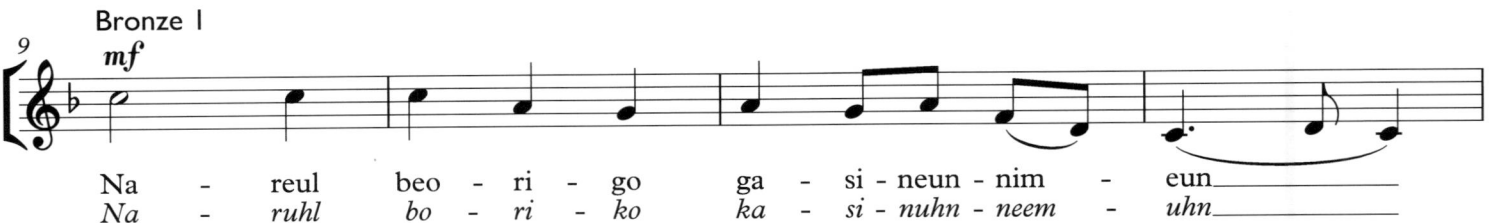

Italicised lyrics show words written phonetically to aid pronunciation.

'Arirang' is a popular Korean folk song about love and longing. It is considered by some to be an unofficial national anthem.

© 2025 by The Associated Board of the Royal Schools of Music

What would it be like?

Words and Music by
Emily Barden

© 2025 by The Associated Board of the Royal Schools of Music

Lullaby

Words and Music by
Niki Davies

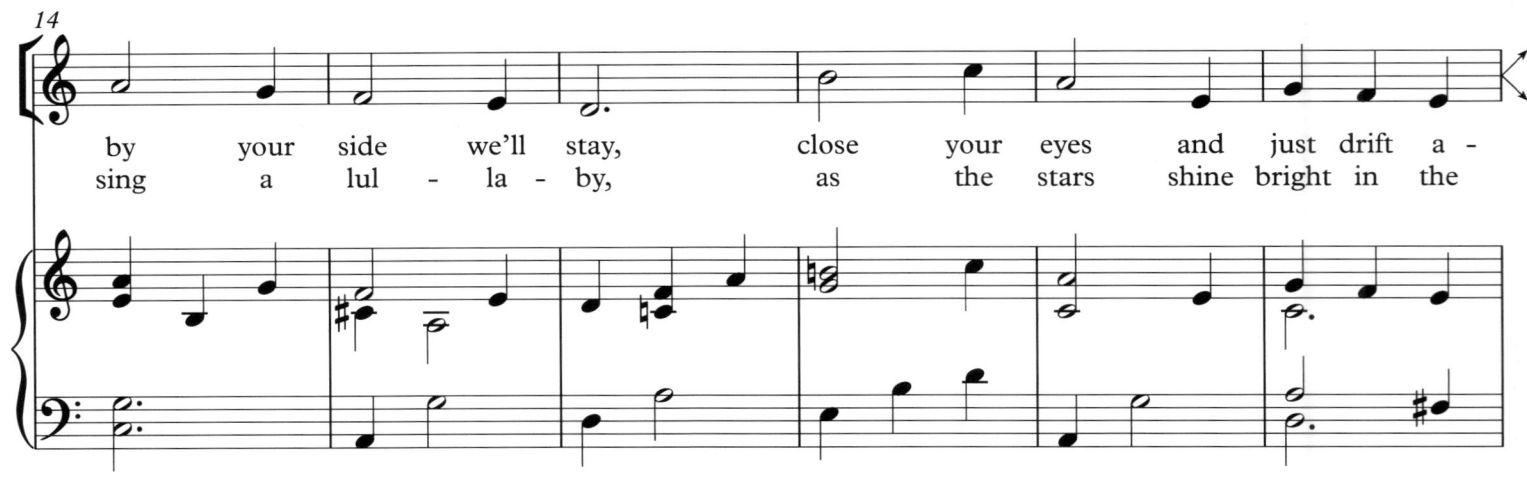

Copyright © 2025 The School Musicals Company Ltd

Perica

Trad. Chilean

* Pronounce 'kyeh'

'Perica' can be a diminutive of the name Petra, but it can also mean a small parrot or parakeet.
To access an audio pronunciation guide, scan the QR code at the front of this book.

© 2025 by The Associated Board of the Royal Schools of Music

I Love Football

Words and Music by
Francis Winston

This rap has been notated on a two-line stave to give a sense of how the voice should be inflected for a stylistic performance. To listen to an audio demo, scan the QR code at the front of this book.

© 2025 by The Associated Board of the Royal Schools of Music

Igama la Bantwana

Trad. South African (Zulu)

* Blur the intervals in a downward glide (*portamento*)

This is a soothing song, sung to a baby whose mother has had to leave her child with another woman – perhaps to go to work. Italicised lyrics show words written phonetically to aid pronunciation. To access an audio pronunciation guide, scan the QR code at the front of this book.

© 2025 by The Associated Board of the Royal Schools of Music